Have you ever wondered how you would happen before it took place? We all receive feelings about things, and many times we're right.

Everyone receives impressions of things. Even mechanics get impressions about the cars they work on. We receive answers to questions from a mysterious place inside us.

In this book we will learn to be more aware of our mysterious impressions and see the *auras* that create them.

My quest for aura sight began in 1973 after having a psychic reading by a clairvoyant. With little hesitation he began a 30-minute session. He gazed at my aura, seeing colors and pictures of my life, past and future. He was direct and at ease as he spoke to me about what he saw and felt. And I was fascinated and amazed by the information.

The clairvoyant was the third of three spiritual teachers I had seen in a time span of four months. The first was an astrologer and the second a medium. All told me my future work was in intuition, communication and innovation, mixed with teaching. I simply needed to choose my path. Because I was so impressed with the clairvoyant, I chose to see and work with the aura as my field of study.

A few weeks after the session with the clairvoyant I saw my first aura.

As anyone with an avid interest in a subject would, I desired "fast-food" wisdom on how to see the aura. But I was left wanting. There were few books on the subject in the early 1970s. I could find only one.

We here in the States are such impatient people. We want *everything* today. I know little about computers, but I write with one and access programs on it. To me it doesn't matter a great deal that I understand binary components or other such things. I just want to know how to use my computer.

The same is true with learning about our inner powers. The great depth of spiritual study attributed to the creation of the energy of the aura can slow down our interest by confusing us with heavy subject matter.

Most books on the subject of auras tend to be full of complexities because the author writes to those readers who already know the subject, not to the mainstream. Hey, what's the big deal, anyway?

Why spend so much time in trivial details? We already have the ability to see the aura, a natural ability we are born with. We have something inside that talks to us and gives us signals. This ability is as natural as breathing, and we rarely pay attention to our breathing patterns.

When it comes to a deep or complex study, most of us would tend to say, "First show me that the thing really exists and how to use it, and *then* tell me the do's and don'ts. If I need to know more later, I'll ask." Now, doesn't this sound right for the majority of us?

Accessing this native ability is what this booklet is all about.

So now let's talk about the do's and don'ts. A basic principle of energy is its natural propensity to become part of a collective, gathered together by magnetic force. Whatever energy the collective body sends out is magnetized and will come back. (Our physical body, our thoughts and emotions, are a collective body.) What goes around, comes around. Send out good vibrations, and we will receive them back.

Invade someone's privacy, and ours will be invaded. Simple enough ground rules for do's and don'ts, wouldn't you say?

Our outside world is a reflection of what's going on within us. The world is our mirror.

Contents

Illustrations

Introduction

The mind is a wondrous tool. It processes information like nothing in this world. And in the processing it selects what to give to the conscious mind and what not to give.

It's rare for the mind to let us see anything that doesn't fit into our everyday experience.

This sounds strange — the mind choosing instead of ourselves. But there is a selective overseer in our mind. This "self" is introduced in the following chapter.

I want to share a story about the mind not seeing what it does not recognize.

When the sailing ships from Europe first appeared in the waters off the South American coastline, few of the local people noticed them. Only the priests saw the ships. They ran to the people and said, "Look! Do you see the large boats?"

But none could see. So then one of the priests said, "Do you see the geese?" And the people said, "Oh yes, we can see the geese."

CHAPTER ONE
Auras

Do you know what an aura is? It describes a certain kind of presence that surrounds or enhances a person, place or thing.

"The aura of the park seemed cold for such a warm evening. He could feel someone or something in the distance watching him."

Does that help you understand a little more?

This presence has been written about for some time. It's like one of those descriptions we can see in our mind as we read, but how can it relate to our everyday life?

Remember back to a time when you caught yourself staring at someone. You might even have gotten a feeling inside about that person, as if you could almost read his mind?

What you sensed (and you did sense it) was that person's aura. It was such a subtle thing, yet full of impact. And subtle means just that.

There is a part of ourselves that is much more observant than we are. It remembers everything, storing the information like a video tape. Its name is Innerself. It records and evaluates everything within its parameter. So naturally it will also observe the aura.

Fulfilling its role as the observant one, Innerself is always busy sorting through incoming information and placing it at the level of importance relative to our desires. It processes all the sound, temperature, lighting and how the body is adapting to its surroundings. Innerself keeps everything running while we focus on the outside world and whatever draws our attention.

There is so much going on around us that to try and pay attention to everything would be impossible. So we need an inner self that does the work behind the scenes.

Innerself is devoted to the conscious mind. It brings to our attention what we desire. It's on the lookout for anything that could hurt or help us. This means it also screens out anything too unusual for us to consciously participate in, things that might disturb or disrupt our normal thinking.

Consciously seeing an aura would disrupt most people's normal way of being. It would cause a great disturbance.

Innerself communicates in different ways for different people. Most hear a voice inside. Many times we've listened and followed along and other times we've chosen not to take its advice.

At the times we chose not to listen, we usually lost in one way or another, even if it was only time off the clock.

Sometimes we yell at ourselves for not listening to our feelings. We struggle too often with decisions, sometimes very simple ones.

Because of the conflict that usually occurs, Innerself has learned through the years to just keep quiet.

It's most important in our study of aura sight to realize and to know that *Innerself is the one that sees,*

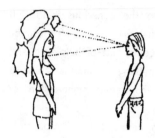

feels, or becomes aware of the aura first. Through this part of us we learn to see consciously and physically.

Simply wanting to see an aura does not make it happen easily. We need to first get past the mind by playing a game that uses our imagination.

Using our imagination allows Innerself the freedom to play along with our desire, and with that freedom we can see.

Experiments have shown that when we quickly "make something up" about an aura in class situations, the conclusion is fairly accurate — sometimes *very* accurate. But the minute a person tries to anticipate and use conscious thought, the flow of aura information stops or goes astray from the reality.

The work of tuning in must begin with a nonchalant attitude that won't judge any ideas or feelings, an attitude that will remain open to impressions in the form of imagination.

Many of us have learned to trust our gut feelings/hunches, haven't we? If we want this inner magic to happen more frequently, then we must give these flashes of insight conscious confirmation when they occur. The easiest way is to say thank you.

We want to build a bridge to the still, small voice within.

How to Spot an Aura

The aura is most easily seen surrounding the rounded areas of the body. Head, shoulders, hands, feet, knees, elbows. These areas give off the most amount of energy radiating from the body, so around the head and shoulders is the best area for viewing the aura.

The halo is the best-known location for aura energy. Many see this without really trying. It is the most documented by theologian, scientist and clairvoyant alike.

In later study one can learn to project the aura energy through these rounded areas of the body. Surprisingly, the elbows and knees can be the most effective.

CHAPTER TWO
How to See

Well now, I bet you're anxious to get started, so let's get right to it.

To begin, let's think about what we do when we daydream. We're usually staring at nothing in particular. We're caught up in another reality of thought, picture and emotion. Reality is right there in front of us, but the imagining is so powerful that it fills our mind and we find ourselves in a waking dream.

When we look at an aura we're seeing differently. We're applying the daydreamer's stare and letting our imagination create a picture of the aura on our mind's eye. We work with our physical eyes to see, *slowly, slowly* letting the aura make its appearance.

The aura has four levels. Each level represents a different expression of us and our body.

These aura expressions show themselves the way we probably expect them to, that is, thoughts that form structures, and emotions flying.

The first level is connected to the physical body. The second level is the emotional aura. The third is the mental aura and the fourth level is the spiritual aura.

But to get started we won't try to see the different levels. We just want to see the bubble and a color or two, nothing too heavy in the beginning. If we try for too much, we can easily be disappointed.

The Bubble

The easiest way to picture the aura is to see it like a bubble. Nothing too much at first, only the outline of a *clear* bubble, a bubble big enough to enclose a body with a radiance 3 to 6 feet from the body in all directions.

It really doesn't matter if you have a particular background to view the aura, although many think so.

It's as easy as pie to do it without a special background.

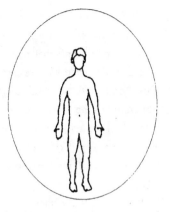

Let me show you an example. Picture in your mind an apple. A red apple. See it? Notice how the mind instantly gave you a picture of the apple. It was probably off in the background of your imagination. It wasn't as clear as being right in front of you, but it was there. Now see in your mind a bubble surrounding someone. You will see it like you saw the apple, in the corner of your mind.

For your information, the farther away the person is, the easier it is to see the bubble. So a person can be 100 yards from you, but if you play with it, you will see the person's bubble quite easily.

Hold this thought: We will most likely see the aura in our mind *before* we see it with our outer sight. Remember, the imagination holds the key. Some workshoppers have made the mistake of expecting to see something without applying their imagination first, and then complained that they didn't get it.

Expecting immediate results without following the steps won't work because you're wanting something to happen that's new to you, and it seldom works like that. Your conscious mind needs time to get used to seeing something it doesn't normally see. So go easy, don't push, and picture the aura in your imagination first.

As mentioned earlier, we certainly don't need a white backdrop and soft lights to do this. But if you feel that you need something like this, then let me suggest a light-colored wall free of objects. Have subdued lighting. Your subject should stand a few feet out from the wall and you should be about 6 feet away. Like the illustration on the next page, look above the head and shoulders.

Using the daydream stare, look above and behind your friend. Keep your stare between your friend and the wall.

Look deep into the distance (of the space between) and take away all third-dimensional objects

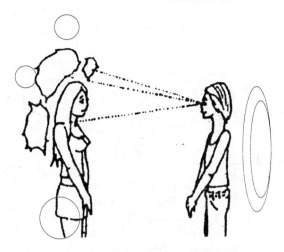

from your focused sight. This stare and the conscious choice to see the aura will trigger the technique and you'll get results.

The hardest thing to do when we first *see* an aura is to detect its color. Our eyes need to be trained to pick up this subtle light, so if you don't see color at first, that's quite normal. You will see a different kind of light, though, a light that's yellow-white, sort of gold, but it really isn't color. It's simply all the un-trained eye can see for the moment.

The Four Stages of Development

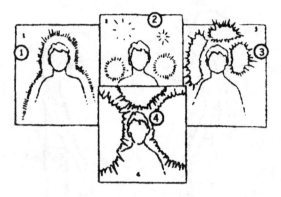

Beginning with step 1 (check the numbers above), we see the etheric body vibrating the Earth's magnetic energy. This etheric energy is not considered an aura level. Although you might see this shadow body almost completely surrounding the physical, it does not reveal the real aura.

The colors normally appear small (2) in the beginning and grow with practice (3 and 4).

CHAPTER THREE

Colors and Their Meanings

Understand color,
and you uncover
the subtleties of the
physical universe.

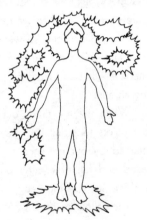

This is the time to talk about colors.

Everything is energy in motion. To our normal perception the world is full of things that appear solid to us, but mathematics has proven that nothing is really solid and that the physical universe is basically simply light/energy in motion. We also know that when energy moves, it creates color according to the speed of its vibrations.

Our physical body is a collection of atoms: particles of energy vibrating between 350,000 to 400,000 light waves per second. We are light in the purest sense. And so we radiate.

We radiate light, so we should imagine our insides as a light bulb with the physical body acting as a lampshade — a subtle radiance projecting outward to create an aura.

When we are tired, our energy slows down and our colors turn dull and gray. People sometimes feel drained by our presence. Conversely, when we feel good and full of energy, our colors are bright, light, and we energize the people we encounter.

The following descriptions of color are held to be universal. If mathematics can prove the existence of matter, then we can assume that energy, when vibrating in a specific range of speed, will have an effect when encountering other energy — sometimes speeding it up, sometimes slowing it down.

This is to say that red creates an effect on other energy, doing only what red can do, and cannot assume the duties of another color. The same is true for all colors. Each color has its own use.

Red: The densest color on the color wheel. Red creates the most friction. Friction attracts and repels. Anger (repelling) is seen in muddied red.

Red is sexy (attracting).

Soft pink is affection.

In a good, bright and pure state, red energy can serve as a healthy ego.

Orange: The color of vitality, vigor, good health and excitement. Lots of energy.

Yellow: The color of awakening. The birth of creativity and inspiration. Intelligent action and intelligence shared. The light bulb above the head in cartoons.

Green: One of the healthy colors of nature and also a very comfortable one. When seen in the aura this usually represents growth and balance, but most of all, something that leads to a change.

Blue: This color is cool, calm, collected. Soft blue: peacefulness, clarity, and communication. Reflects a high spirituality when seen in a sapphire glimmer.

Purple: The most sensitive and wisest of colors on the wheel. This is the intuitive color in the aura and reveals psychic power of attunement with self.

Silver: This is the color of abundance, both spiritual and physical. Lots of bright silver refers to plenty of money. And it also refers to the awakening cosmic mind.

Gold: This is the color of enlightenment and divine protection. When seen within the aura, it says that the person is being guided by her highest good, and in most you will see a willing follower. It is divine guidance.

Black: Draws/pulls energy to it and in so doing, transforms it. It captures light and consumes it.

White: Reflects other energy. A pure state of light. It will represent a new, not yet designated energy in the aura.

Earth colors: Soil, wood, mineral, plant. These colors display a love of the Earth, of being grounded and is seen in those who live and work in the outdoors — construction, farming, etc. These colors are important and are a good sign.

Pastels: A sensitive blend of light and color, more so than basic colors. Shows sensitivity and serenity.

CHAPTER FOUR
The Body Centers
Everyday meanings of the energy centers
we call chakras

There are areas of the body that reveal more of the daily silent goings-on of a person (silent meaning behind the scenes, internal arousals or disturbances).

These areas are called, to use a spiritual and metaphysical term, *chakras*, an East Indian word for wheel.

I don't feel a need to go into all the high spiritual stuff about the chakras, because if someone is interested in a broader study, the information is easily available through a number of books on the subject.

These centers are valid and important in *displaying our reactions to everyday life*, and for this reason I include this material here.

Once we are aware of the aura by seeing a bubble, many impressions of color will show up all over the bubble, some appearing over the chakras. Therefore the reader also needs this knowledge . I mean to simplify the information for the reader yet still provide useful material.

The centers we will discuss are throughout the body, following the spine from one end to the other. There are seven (7) of these and each has its own design and purpose.

It is best to envision a whirlpool of energy, a spinning wheel, when considering what to look for in our mind's eye. After practice we will begin to see the whirlpools in different designs and symbolic forms that will lead us to an understanding of what's going on.

Let's begin with the lowest chakra. This area is the procreative zone, our place of passion. When this area is lit up, we are filled with passion, good or bad. The color seen for this area is red: attraction and repulsion.

There will be times when we will see a different color over the area instead of its designated color. Let's say we see gray-green in the pro-creative zone. This tells us there is unbalance in the person's health. If we see pur-ple, intuition is playing a part within that center. A gray-red shows a problem with self-esteem.

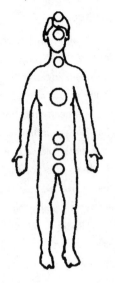

The second center is the color orange, designated as the health and vitality center of the body. (It has been called by some the sexual center.) The degree of orange we see shows the de-gree of vitality. Bright orange denotes an energetic person.

Then there will be days when we see a dull orange with burnt edges. Simply said, the person's energy is burned out.

Covering the stomach area is the third center, and

its color is yellow. Surprisingly, this is where we experience intuitive and creative flashes (gut feelings). The Innerself will project its insight from this spot. Not conscious ideas as the mind would, but insightful monitoring of our overall self.

The heart, the fourth center, is the place where we find understanding and balance. At its highest, balance finds blessed unity with kindred spirits, and the desire to find completeness in another fills us. We are drawn like moths to a flame and spend all our waking moments imaging bliss with that special person.

Although the color for this center is green, the one most always associated with the heart is red. We are attraction city. We are hot to trot. We are ready for love.

But then of course there are times when other colors associated with the heart will be seen. "Green with envy" and "feeling blue." And let's not forget about those "black-hearted demons" disguised as people. You know who I'm talking about. Those who have "Beware" written all over everything they breathe on or touch, the person or persons who would have you eaten alive before breakfast each day of the week if they could. The next time you happen to cross their path or they yours, check out their heart.

The fifth center covers the throat and is the color blue. Our communication flows from this center. Seeing the everyday situations from this spot, the color will reveal whether a person is open to or holding back from whomever they need to speak to or whatever needs to be said.

One of the funny symbols I have noticed is this: ∅ — the "no-way" sign. This symbol will no doubt be seen covering other centers also, as it refers to that center's energy.

Of course, seeing energy over the throat can show a sore throat or cold, but remember to take into consideration that the body tends to act out feelings through ill health. So you see the color and you think, "This person is covering up something," but you hear the person complaining about his throat. You might want to look a little deeper into the chakra itself for the answer.

I remind and caution you that prying too deeply into matters that are not your concern can be troublesome to you later on.

The sixth center is the color purple. It has been called the mystic eye, the third eye, the mind's eye, the inner screen and so forth. It displays images, ideas that flash in front of the mind, ideas that can be envisioned with increased clarity when our eyes are closed and not distracted by the outside world.

This center lets us see that someone is looking at the world inside out. If there is a murky color, then there is depression or lack of faith in how he sees his life in the present.

Here is another way to read the centers. If you see half of the center covered with a different color, then things are changing, either past to future or in the present time. Get it? The person is undergoing some kind of change in how he views the world. This can be very positive.

Seeing this center's energy will also show us the level of people's awareness, how insightful/intuitive they are. It displays their ability to envision and receive psychic visions. The bigger the center, the more power there is to project and use.

The high spot of all the chakras is called the crown because that is where it's located. In this area we see the general disposition of the individual — for instance, whether the present intake of energy is good, bad or indifferent or if the energy is a continuance from the past, is changing now, or is brand new.

The color green seen above the head points to a change manifesting itself in the present for that person. This change will also be reflected in other areas of the aura bubble, and it is up to us to locate them.

CHAPTER FIVE
Examples of Everyday Auras

Lisa has been troubled lately. We see the darker shape above the shoulder indicating her mental state over a problem, and her emotions reveal that the problem concerns something she loves. According to the energy pattern, this situation could last awhile.

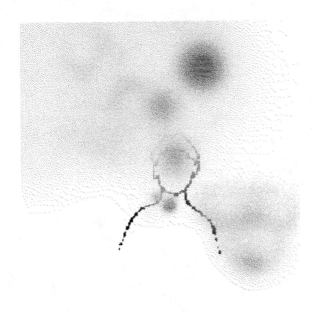

John sees a great opportunity to move ahead in business and he is close to voicing his ideas. As we can see, the near future looks good for his emotions and everyday life.

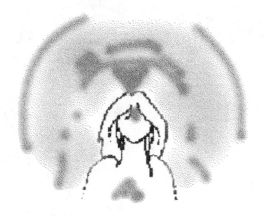

Lisa is being shy. A soft basic blue of coolness and protection overshadows the warm, attractive pink, and she purposely blocks out her thoughts and feelings.

A very exhausting and trying day for John. His aura is dull and heavy. His thoughts and emotions are overwhelmed by his physical aura.

Lisa is expressing some very positive thoughts and feelings. Her colors are red, green, and yellow. Soft colors, but very vibrant.

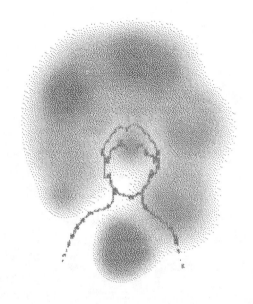

John is being the madman. He's angry. He's seeing red. His aura is heavy with gray, muddy red.

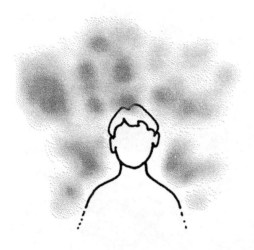

John is having a creative idea concerning his business. Yellow and silver appear to flash above his head and a clear, charged-up blue beams from his shoulders, suggesting that he can feel the inspiration.

Lisa feels rejected by her lover and at the same time very defensive. Surrounding her head and shoulders is a blackened edge of rose-pink. She places in front of her heart a shield of cold blue.

Now, I realize that showing you aura examples without color is a disappointment, but when we first begin seeing aura energy, it's usually only in shadow form anyway, like a film negative.

The image can appear easily in the beginning, but the makeup of the image might be colorless and fuzzier than we would like. We have to work hard, sometimes struggle, to bring in the full picture. This requires imagination, and honesty, too. (True seeing requires honesty — there are lots of hits and misses — and a constant desire to improve. Without this honesty we can be nothing more than party entertainers.) Ask yourself for the color and see if it begins to appear as you stare at the area in the aura.

Use practice sheets and color them. The figures are supplied on page 59. This will improve your talent.

CHAPTER SIX

Reading the Vibrations

Understanding what you see in the Aura

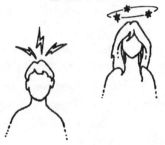

When we see an aura, remember that it's seeing an entire bubble complete in light.

In the common past of aura reading, one looked straight at a subject to see energy above the head and shoulders and even at the sides. But in today's presentation the reader will also notice energy in front of the person, looking for color that covers the upper torso. (See the illustration on page 37.)

So as we look, we see a patchwork of color throughout the bubble. Why a patchwork? Because we are seeing four levels of the aura at once, with different levels having precedence over others.

There are times when we place more importance on thinking than gut feelings, and this shows in the aura. I have provided a chart to show you how to distinguish one level from the other (see illustration on pg. 40).

Let's go another step further and talk about seeing timing within the bubble. Yes, I said timing — the past, present and future from the colors we see.

How can we do that? How can we actually see things occurring days, months and even years before or after present time from the aura?

The body and its energies conform to the magnetic energies of the Earth. This magnetic energy flows clockwise from the equator to the North Pole. It flows counterclockwise from the equator to the South Pole. In this way we begin to see time.

Energy circulates, flowing to us, bringing our future thoughts and actions. And as it leaves, it displays the record of what has occurred.

A Patchwork of Color

So those of us in the U.S., for instance, have our future at our left, the present above us and the past to the right. It would be the opposite for those in Australia, whose future would be seen to the right.

We judge time by the distance of the color from the body (see illustration pg. 43). In my 20-plus years of research, I have discovered a very simple technique to distinguish the timing: Sort through the four energy levels and allow them all to be seen at once — a momentary freeze-frame.

This technique has been applied by many over the twelve years of workshops and has proven itself time and again to be accurate.

Now, what about the technique, and how do we do it? The easiest way to explore this technique is to use some tools. The tools are scratch paper and either crayons or colored pencils, and 24 colors serve best.

I suggest that the drawing be done without thinking about the choice of color or where it will be placed on the paper.

I stress this for a reason. It won't be the conscious mind that does the coloring. Or at least it shouldn't be, because trying to think this through will keep the real aura from showing. *Trying* to color the aura screws it up. How can we possibly leave this "seeing" to a part of us that hasn't done it? The conscious mind has most likely never attempted an exercise like this and would fall short.

So again, the best way is to play along and *make up* our drawing/coloring as quickly as we can without hesitation. We do it without trying, without trying to decide the color we want to use or where to place it.

Let's go back to the illustration and instructions concerning viewing the aura (pages 10 and 11). Using the same position for the person whose aura will be drawn, find a table to work on and a chair to sit in. Spread the colors out so they'll be easy to select and pick up. We start by taking a nice calming breath.

Aura levels are now seen in a different perspective from past instruction. This new look is considered more versatile yet still accurate.

We now gaze at the aura for just a few moments, quickly up and down the body. We tell ourselves to color the aura in front of us. We look down at the paper and begin. It works best if we don't look back at our subjects until we're finished. Trust the game.

Spiritual   Spiritual

Mental   Mental

Day-to-Day   Day-to-Day

Emotional   Emotional

Physical   Physical

The horizontal layers

You know, if you try to get too cutesy with your drawing, you'll miss the opportunity to see all the areas I share in this instruction. Please don't think about how you have seen an aura from the interpretation of others (lines surrounding the body), just scribble all over the sheet of paper.

The technique and our opportunity to physically

see another's aura work hand in hand. It was only after many colorings that I discovered all that I had been missing in the aura by using only my second sight.

I needed to include my feeling perception to complete my reading. My first months using the coloring proved to be very beneficial. In discovering for myself the technique, I saw colors I hadn't seen in the past. This opened another major door in my education.

As we practice, we gain. The benefits lie in the doing. Whenever you get the urge, grab some colors and go to it. This is really easy to do while you talk to someone over the telephone. It's just like doodling. Keep some scratch paper and a jar of colored pencils or crayons close to the telephone you use the most, and as you move into your conversation, begin picking up the colors and draw.

The unusual, mysterious, interesting and funny thing is *how* we color. Sometimes we will apply more pressure on the color to make it darker; the same goes for the softness of our strokes. The circles and lines also matter. This is the mystery of our inner mind. From somewhere inside we know, and this translates onto the paper.

Consider the progression of the colors past to future. Also notice the energy that surrounds the hands and feet. This points to what we are letting go of as well as what we seek to accept from our future. Only one image appears at a time, and it will not necessarily be in an ordered sequence. Once we begin to see something in the aura and hold the image in our thought, we move our vision quickly, scanning back and forth across the bubble until we see another area light up or appear.

This new thing should be the connection we are looking for. Depending whether it falls in the past or future, we look at the opposite to see the rest of the story.

On the next page is a time chart, but as you can see, it can reveal many things to us.

When we deal with just one matter important to the subject, although other levels of the aura will show us a more complete picture, we can see the present influences in the subject's life.

1. We look into her past for a connection. In the area of her mental aura we see a corresponding color/shape that entered into her thinking about three or four months ago.

2. Looking now to the future in her day-to-day life, we see how it will give birth to more of the same. If all goes well, before six months are up, lots of new things will happen.

Time Chart, the Vertical Layers

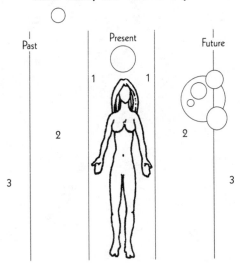

1: Present to two weeks
2: Two weeks to six months
3: Six months to one+ year

CHAPTER SEVEN

The Symbols

There is a group of symbols that provides a special technique to train our eyes to see the subtle vibrations of light and color. They are called symbols rather than shapes because each one of the first four were used in ancient mystery schools for precisely the same reason we will use them today.

To receive the full impact of these symbols, it is suggested that we hold one at arm's length and stare at it for 15 seconds without blinking, then remove it from our direct vision and look straight ahead.

We will see an afterimage of the symbol (the color

is opposite) floating in front of us. Hold that image as long as possible. Practice with the same symbol a couple of times before moving on to the next.

What you witness is the semblance of the aura colors as they will appear surrounding some person or thing. Not everyone will see all the colors at first, but practice a lot and soon you will.

Use one or all of the symbols prior to exercising your aura sight. It sensitizes and prepares the eyes. You might try holding it in front of your subject and then after removal, the color will appear to surround him/her/it.

CHAPTER EIGHT
Review: The Steps to Seeing

In the beginning use the colored symbols to sensitize your eyes.

1. Now let your imagination envision a bubble. Is it heavy, light, big or small?

2. Gaze above the head and shoulders and imagine three colors, one over each shoulder and one above the head. The color above the head shows what is now; above the shoulders shows what has been and where it's going.

3. If you have trouble seeing anything close around the head (faces can be distracting), take your vision about 3 or 4 feet above or to the side. Sometimes it's much easier to see these areas. Similarly, you can concentrate on the energy from the feet or hands.

For your study and enjoyment I have provided the two figures on the next page. If you wish, make several larger copies. Cut them in half, gluing each figure to separate sheets of paper. Now you can practice with them.

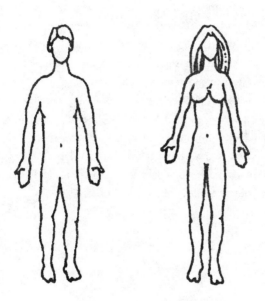

Gabriel Hudson Bain has been involved with the study and application of auras and their energies since 1974. He has twenty years of working experience as a professional psychic counselor, including twelve years of teaching successful workshops on developing the ability to see and sense the aura.

Gabriel is a celebrity psychic, having appeared on several shows, both television and radio, and has received write-ups in both magazine and newspapers.

Through the years Gabriel has developed a strong clairvoyant psychic ability and shares his knowledge with others through lectures and private sessions.

Contact Gabriel at
auras101@sedona.net

We offer answers to satisfy the
heart and mind

SEDONA
Journal of EMERGENCE!

8.5" X 11", MONTHLY
128p, PERFECT BOUND
$5.95 U.S.A. / $7.50 Canada

"There is something for every mental fabric along
metaphysical lines in the *Sedona
Journal of EMERGENCE!*,
and people are gradually
going back to that thing that
feeds the heart, that tells them
there's a reason for it all.
So the whole message
ultimately of the *Sedona
Journal* is the simple,
warm-hearted rendition of the 'truth'."

— Zoosh/Robert Shapiro

DON'T SPECULATE . . . GET SOURCE INFORMATION!

**THE LATEST
COSMIC HEADLINE
NEWS!**
ETs, Secret
Government, Earth
Changes, Great
Channels,
PREDICTABLES
Dimensional Shift, the
Photon Belt . . .
and More!

ORDER NOW!
**before subscription rates are raised!
New Cover Price $5.95**

The one monthly magazine readers never throw away . . .
helps you open spiritual doors to new dimensions of
awareness.

The latest channeled information on what to do as humans
and the Earth move from the third to the fourth dimension
— how these energies affect you and the Earth.

Practical articles and features on New Age humor, healing,
children's stories, ETs, UFOs, astrology, herbs, numerology,
reincarnation and more!

WHAT YOU NEED TO KNOW NOW AS YOU AND EARTH CHANGE

Light Technology Publishing Presents

THE EXPLORER RACE SERIES

the EXPLORER RACE

Zoosh, End-Time Historian
through Robert Shapiro

The Origin...
The Purpose...
The Future of
Humanity...

Zoosh & Others through Robert Shapiro

"After all the words that we put out, ultimately the intention is to persuade people's minds, otherwise known as giving their minds the answers that their minds hunger for so that their minds can get out of the way and let their hearts take them to where they would naturally go anyway." – Zoosh/Robert Shapiro

THE SERIES

Humans — creators in training — have a purpose and destiny so heart-warmingly, profoundly glorious that it is almost unbelievable from our present dimensional perspective. Humans are great lightbeings from beyond this creation, gaining experience in dense physicality. This truth about the great human genetic experiment of the Explorer Race and the mechanics of creation is being revealed for the first time by Zoosh and his friends through superchannel Robert Shapiro. These books read like adventure stories as we follow the clues from this creation that we live in out to the Council of Creators and beyond.

THE EXPLORER RACE SERIES

❶ the EXPLORER RACE

This book presents humanity in a new light, as the explorers and problem-solvers of the universe, admired by the other galactic beings for their courage and creativity. Some topics are: The Genetic Experiment on Earth; The ET in You: Physical Body, Emotion, Thought and Spirit; The Joy, the Glory and the Challenge of Sex; ET Perspectives; The Order: Its Origin and Resolution; Coming of Age in the Fourth Dimension and much more!

574p $25.00

❷ ETs and the EXPLORER RACE

In this book Robert channels Joopah, a Zeta Reticulan now in the ninth dimension, who continues the story of the great experiment — the Explorer Race — from the perspective of his race. The Zetas would have been humanity's future selves had not humanity re-created the past and changed the future.
237p $14.95

❸ Origins and the Next 50 Years

Some chapters are: THE ORIGINS OF EARTH RACES: Our Creator and Its Creation, The White Race and the Andromedan Linear Mind, The Asian Race, The African Race, The Fairy Race and the Native Peoples of the North, The Australian Aborigines, The Origin of Souls. THE NEXT 50 YEARS: The New Corporate Model, The Practice of Feeling, Benevolent Magic, Future Politics, A Visit to the Creator of All Creators. ORIGINS OF THE CREATOR: Creating with Core Resonances; Jesus, the Master Teacher; Recent Events in Explorer Race History; On Zoosh, Creator and the Explorer Race.   339p $14.95

THE EXPLORER RACE SERIES

❹ EXPLORER RACE: Creators and Friends — the Mechanics of Creation

As we explore the greater reality beyond our planet, our galaxy, our dimension, our creation, we meet prototypes, designers, shape-makers, creators, creators of creators and friends of our Creator, who explain their roles in this creation and their experiences before and beyond this creation. As our awareness expands about the way creation works, our awareness of who we are expands and we realize that a part of ourselves is in that vast creation — and that we are much greater and more magnificent than even science fiction had led us to believe. Join us in the adventure of discovery. It's mind-stretching!

435p $19.95

❺ EXPLORER RACE: Particle Personalities

All around you in every moment you are surrounded by the most magical and mystical beings. They are too small for you to see as single individuals, but in groups you know them as the physical matter of your daily life. Particles who might be considered either atoms or portions of atoms consciously view the vast spectrum of reality, yet also have a sense of personal memory like your own linear memory. These particles remember where they have been and what they have done in their infinitely long lives. Some of the particles we hear from are Gold, Mountain Lion, Liquid Light, Uranium, the Great Pyramid's Capstone, This Orb's Boundary, Ice and Ninth-Dimensional Fire. 237p $14.95

THE
EXPLORER
RACE
SERIES

EXPLORER RACE: EXPLORER RACE and BEYOND

In our continuing exploration of how creation works, we talk to Creator of Pure Feelings and Thoughts, the Liquid Domain, the Double-Diamond Portal, and the other 93% of the Explorer Race. We revisit the Friends of the Creator to discuss their origin and how they see the beyond; we finally reach the root seeds of the Explorer Race (us!) and find we are from a different source than our Creator and have a different goal; and we end up talking to All That Is! 360p $14.95

EXPLORER RACE AND BEYOND

Explorer Race Roots, Friends, and All That Is with Zoosh through Robert Shapiro

---

AVAILABLE MID-1998 . . .

EXPLORER RACE and ISIS

Isis sets the record straight on her interaction with humans — what she set out to do and what actually happened. $14.95

COMING SOON

Ⓐ EXPLORER RACE: Material Mastery Series

Secret shamanic techniques to heal particular energy points on Earth, which then feeds healing energy back to humans. $14.95

LIGHT TECHNOLOGY PUBLISHING

HOT OFF THE PRESS

NEW BOOKS!

SHIFTING FREQUENCIES
Jonathan Goldman

A book that gives techniques and meditations to learn to shift our frequency, thereby avoiding the effects of daily bombardments that shift us unwittingly, and enhancing the effects of the incoming assistance. Ultimately we can assist our response to new encodements of light and love raining down/flowing through our planet now.

Jonathan gives international workshops in the field of healing with sound, teaching people how to voice overtones — harmonics on upper and lower registers — for meditations and healing.

$14.95 Softcover 140p   ISBN 1-891824-04-X

SEDONA STARSEED
Raymond Mardyks

A unique constellation of messages from galactic beings focusing on Sedona, as the leading edge of Earth's sweep into an interstellar consciousness. Beings now perceived as star groups — Andromeda, Pleiades, Taurus, Sirius, Lyra and dozens more — offer insights into the connections between the energies of the stars and locations in Sedona. A fascinating exploration of archetypes expressing through the beautiful Sedona geography.

$14.95 Softcover 145p   ISBN 0-9644180-0-2

AURAS 101
A Basic Study of Human Auras and the Techniques to See Them

Gabriel Hudson Bain (Clairvoyant)

An excellent and easy-to-read guide to seeing and understanding auras, the subtle-energy fields that are part of every living being. This book is well-illustrated and leads one easily through simple exercises and explanations into perceiving the aura and knowing what the colors and designs mean. A real value!

$6.95 Softcover 4.25" by 5.5" 60p   ISBN 1-891824-07-4

LIGHT TECHNOLOGY PUBLISHING

HOT OFF THE PRESS

NEW BOOKS!

1-800-GOD-HELP-ME
A LOVE STORY
Michael Farkas

This is one man's story of light, love, ecstasy and creation to help those who need God's direct toll-free line for guidance and instruction on how to make the transition from a life of crisis, filled with drama and difficulty, to a life of constant bliss and evolution. In other words, the how-to-do-it book of joyful metamorphosis.

This guide will be extremely valuable to those who
- are desperate and in serious trouble physically, financially or spiritually and can't wait any longer for the right doctor, "big deal" opportunity or medicine man to show up;
- feel as though they don't have the stamina to last a second longer and are in a real emergency and will soon expire;
- can't afford to be put on hold any longer and must have a direct line to the Creator so they can live wonderfully;
- have experienced the worst possible thing that can happen to a person and no longer find anything funny or happy about life;
- want to learn the principles of wealth and well-being.

$15.95 Softcover 435p   ISBN 1-891824-08-2

WELCOME TO PLANET EARTH
A GUIDE FOR WALK-INS, STARSEEDS AND LIGHTWORKERS OF ALL VARIETIES
Hannah Beaconsfield

Defines and clarifies the walk-in process with examples and channeled information from *the Pleiadian Light* and others. Packed with wide-ranging insight on the world of starseeds and lightworkers; how to deal with difficult issues such as reincarnational depression, transitional trials, fragmented selves and cross-gender replacement. Very informative and enjoyable.

$14.95 Softcover 190p   ISBN 0-929385-98-5

LIGHT TECHNOLOGY PUBLISHING

The Easy-to-Read Encyclopedia of the Spiritual Path

by Dr. Joshua David Stone

A Comprehensive Series on Ascension

THE COMPLETE ASCENSION MANUAL
How to Achieve Ascension in This Lifetime
A synthesis of the past and guidance for ascension. An extraordinary compendium of practical techniques and spiritual history. Compiled from research and channeled information.
$14.95 Softcover 297p   ISBN 0-929385-55-1

SOUL PSYCHOLOGY Keys to Ascension
Modern psychology deals exclusively with personality, ignoring the dimensions of spirit and soul. This book provides ground-breaking theories and techniques for healing and self-realization.
$14.95 Softcover 276p ISBN 0-929385-56-X

BEYOND ASCENSION How to Complete the Seven Levels of Initiation
Brings forth new channeled material that demystifies the 7 levels of initiation and how to attain them. It contains new information on how to open and anchor our 36 chakras.
$14.95 Softcover 279p   ISBN 0-929385-73-X

HIDDEN MYSTERIES
An Overview of History's Secrets from Mystery Schools to ET Contacts
Explores the unknown and suppressed aspects of Earth's past; reveals new information on the ET movement and secret teachings of the ancient Master schools.
$14.95 Softcover 333p ISBN 0-929385-57-8

THE ASCENDED MASTERS LIGHT THE WAY
Keys to Spiritual Mastery from Those Who Achieved It
Lives and teachings of 40 of the world's greatest saints and spiritual beacons provide a blueprint for total self-realization. Guidance from masters.
$14.95 Softcover 258p   ISBN 0-929385-58-6

NEW!!!

COSMIC ASCENSION
Your Cosmic Map Home
Cosmic Ascension is now available here on Earth! Learn about Cosmic Ascension Seats, Monadic Ascension, Self-Realization, Accountability, Cosmic Golden Nuggets, Twelve Planetary Festivals, Cosmic Discipleship and more.
$14.95 Softcover 270p
ISBN 0-929385-99-3

COMING in 1998

• A Beginner's Guide to the Path of Ascension
• Revelations of Sai Baba and the Ascended Masters
• Manual for Planetary Leadership
• Your Ascension Mission: Embracing Your Puzzle Piece
• Revelations of a Melchizedek Initiate

STARCHILD PRESS

A DIVISION OF LIGHT TECHNOLOGY PUBLISHING

for kids of all ages!

THE LITTLE ANGEL BOOKS by LEIA STINNETT

A CIRCLE OF ANGELS
A workbook. An in-depth teaching tool with exercises and illustrations throughout.
$18.95 (8.5" x 11")
ISBN 0-929385-87-X

THE 12 UNIVERSAL LAWS
A workbook for all ages. Learning to live the Universal Laws; exercises and illustrations throughout.
$18.95 (8.5" x 11")
ISBN 0-929385-81-0

ALL MY ANGEL FRIENDS
A coloring book and illustrative learning tool about the angels who lovingly watch over us.
$10.95 (8.5" x 11")
ISBN 929385-80-2

WHERE IS GOD?
Story of a child who finds God in himself and teaches others.
$6.95 ISBN 0-929385-90-X

HAPPY FEET
A child's guide to foot reflexology, with pictures to guide. $6.95
ISBN 0-929385-88-8

WHEN THE EARTH WAS NEW
Teaches ways to protect and care for our Earth.
$6.95 ISBN 0-929385-91-8

THE ANGEL TOLD ME TO TELL YOU GOOD-BYE
Near-death experience heals his fear. $6.95
ISBN 0-929385-84-5

COLOR ME ONE
Lessons in competition, sharing and separateness.
$6.95 ISBN 0-929385-82-9

ONE RED ROSE
Explores discrimination, judgment, and the unity of love.
$6.95 ISBN 0-929385-83-7

ANIMAL TALES
Learning about unconditional love, community, patience and change from nature's best teachers, the animals.
$7.95 ISBN 0-929385-96-9

THE BRIDGE BETWEEN TWO WORLDS
Comfort for the "Star Children" on Earth.
$6.95 ISBN 0-929385-85-3

EXPLORING THE CHAKRAS
Ways to balance energy and feel healthy.
$6.95 ISBN 0-929385-86-1

CRYSTALS FOR KIDS
Workbook to teach the care and properties of stones.
$6.95
ISBN 0-929385-92-6

JUST LIGHTEN UP!
Playful tools to help you lighten up and see the humor in all experiences you create.
$9.95 (8.5" x 11")
ISBN 0-929385-64-0

WHO'S AFRAID OF THE DARK?
Fearful Freddie learns to overcome with love.
$6.95 ISBN 0-929385-89-6

LIGHT TECHNOLOGY PUBLISHING

EASY ORDER

Order ONLINE!
http://www.
sedonajo.com
E-mail:
sedonajo@sedonajo.com

Order by Mail
Send to:
Light Technology Publishing
P.O. Box 1526
Sedona, AZ 86339

Order by Phone
800-450-0985

Order by Fax
520-282-4130

Visit our online bookstore
http://www.sedonajo.com

Secure Transactions
Shopping Cart
Browse at Home

Want in-depth information
on books?
Excerpts and/or reviews of any book
in our book market

STARCHILD PRESS
Wonderful books for children
of all ages, including the Little
Angel Books, coloring books
and books with beautiful full-color art and
great stories.

Journal of EMERGENCE!

Sample channeled excerpts and predictions.
Includes subscription and back-issue
information and order forms.

If you're not online yet,
call Fax on Demand
for catalog info, order form and
in-depth information **800-393-7017**

VISA
MasterCard
NOVUS

WEB SITE/ONLINE BOOKSTORE
OPEN 24 HOURS A DAY